Our Father's Plan

ISBN: 987-0-9976951-6-8

For all our little ones.

Not so long ago, in a place without night,
we lived with our Father, a God full of light.
Without pain or sorrow, we lived in great bliss.
But there was much more to learn — so much joy we would miss.

Our Father in Heaven knew what we could become.
But we needed to grow.
Something had to be done.

He created a plan—and an earth full of life.
A place we could visit to learn love and joy—and
struggle and strife.

Adam and Eve were placed first on this Earth.
They lived in a garden, unaware of their worth.
Father gave them commandments, with a choice to obey.
They were free to explore and choose their own way.

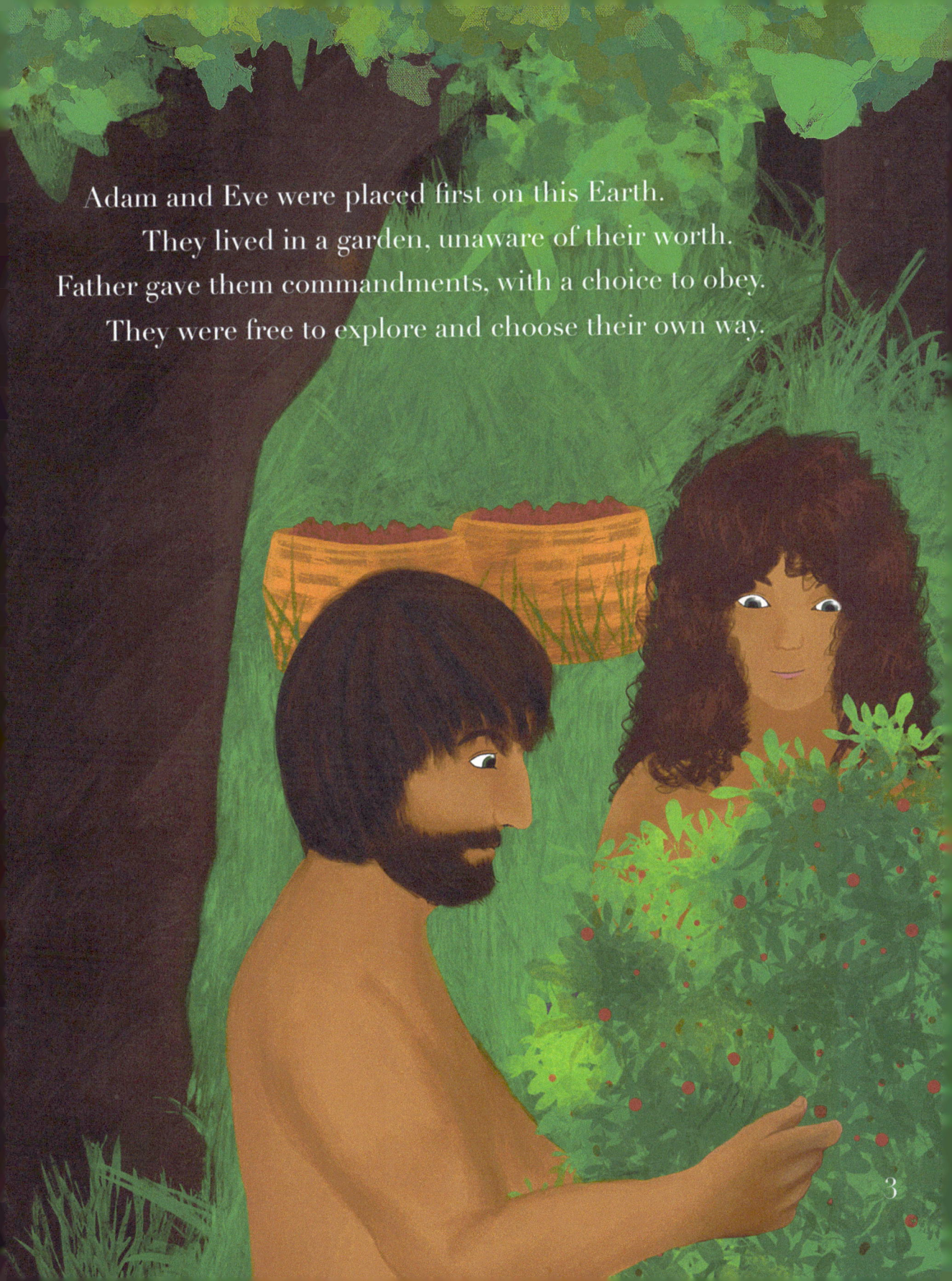

3

Little by little, their family grew,
until the whole world filled with people like you.

We're born here on Earth to test our devotion,

and all throughout life, Father's plan is in motion.

We gain earthly bodies that grow, age, and die,

and the truths that we learn here can help us know why.

Father sends us His gospel
to show us the way
to return to His presence
together someday.
He sends us His spirit to
warn, comfort, and guide.

We talk to Him
through prayer to
thank, ask, and
confide.

If we follow His lead,
He'll guide us along
life's most wonderful paths,
and help us grow strong.

He pours out His blessings
when we choose to follow,
and when we ignore Him,
life is clouded and hollow.

Our true home is heaven, a place without stain.

A haven where no imperfect thing can remain.

So how can we, with our mistakes and our scars,

ever hope to return to the home that was ours?

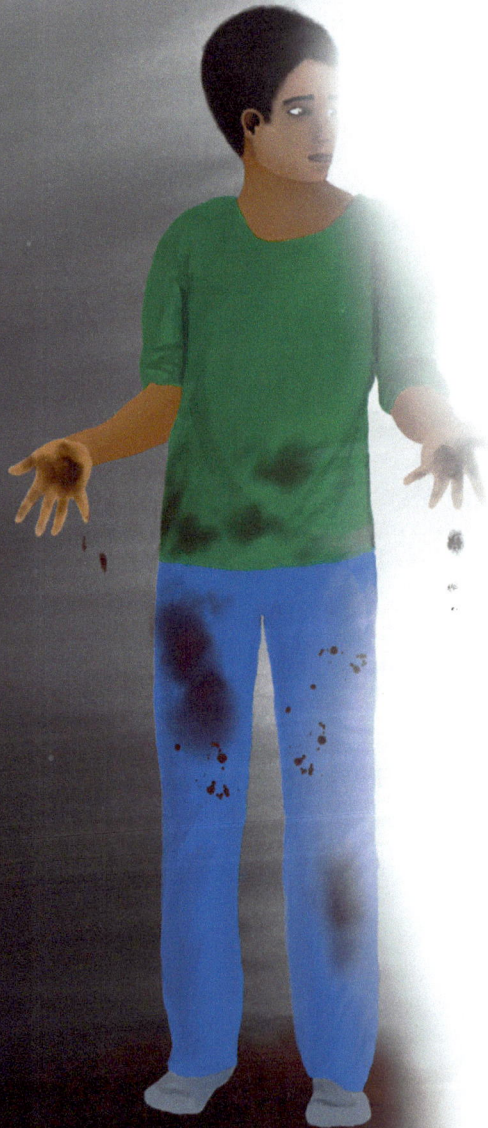

Our Father in Heaven knew
we'd stumble and fall, so He
sent His eldest Son, the
humblest of all.

Jesus Christ came to Earth,
as all of us do. He brought
wonders and taught Father's
gospel anew.

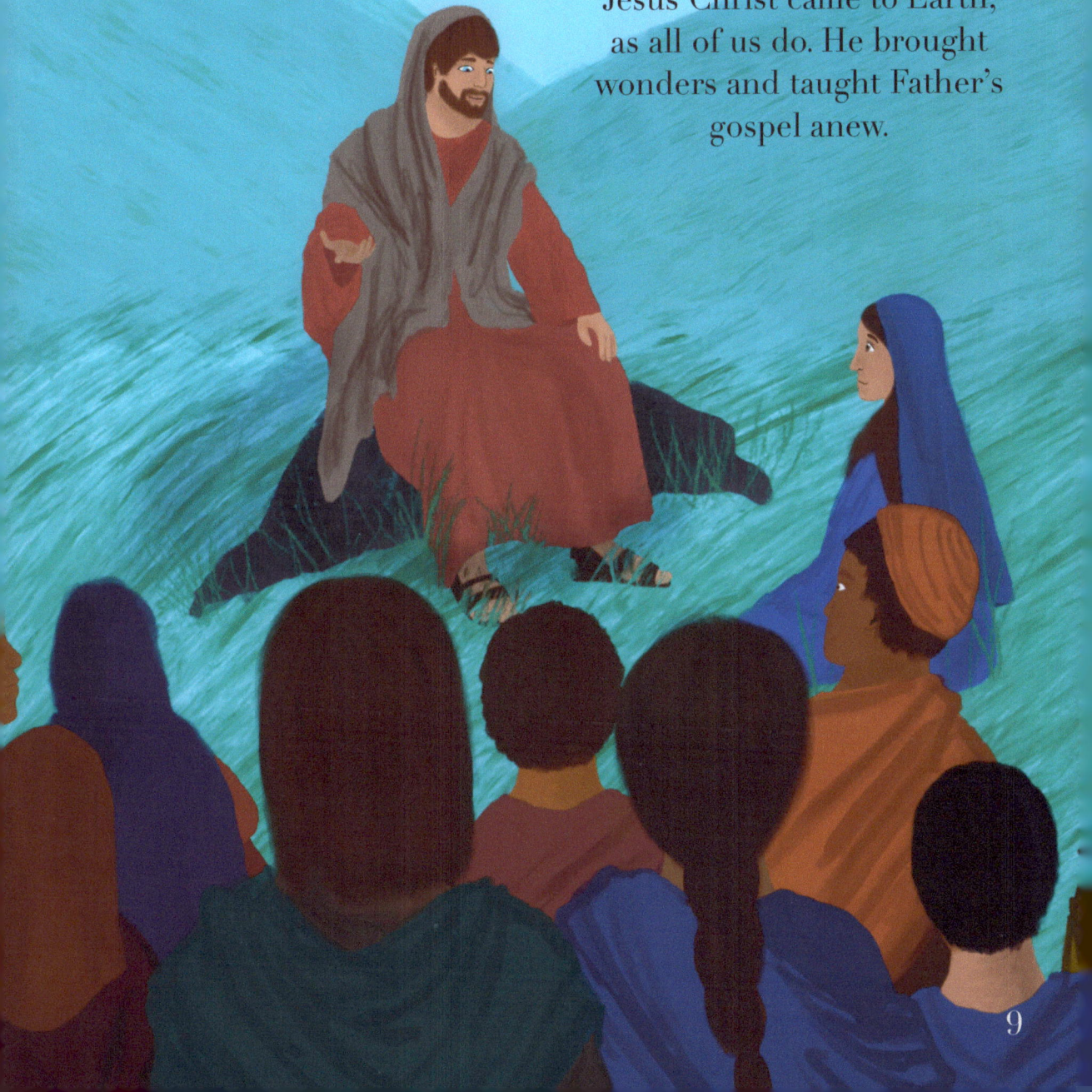

And He gave a gift of immeasurable worth:
He felt all the pains of all people on Earth.
He knows how to heal us, since He's felt it all—
and He helps us grow stronger when life makes us fall.

10

As we trust in Him, His love makes us pure.
When we're baptized, we promise our faith will endure.
And when sins and mistakes leave our hearts full of sorrow,
Jesus helps us repent and have faith in tomorrow.

11

He died for us—then conquered death too.
He rose from the grave with His body renewed.

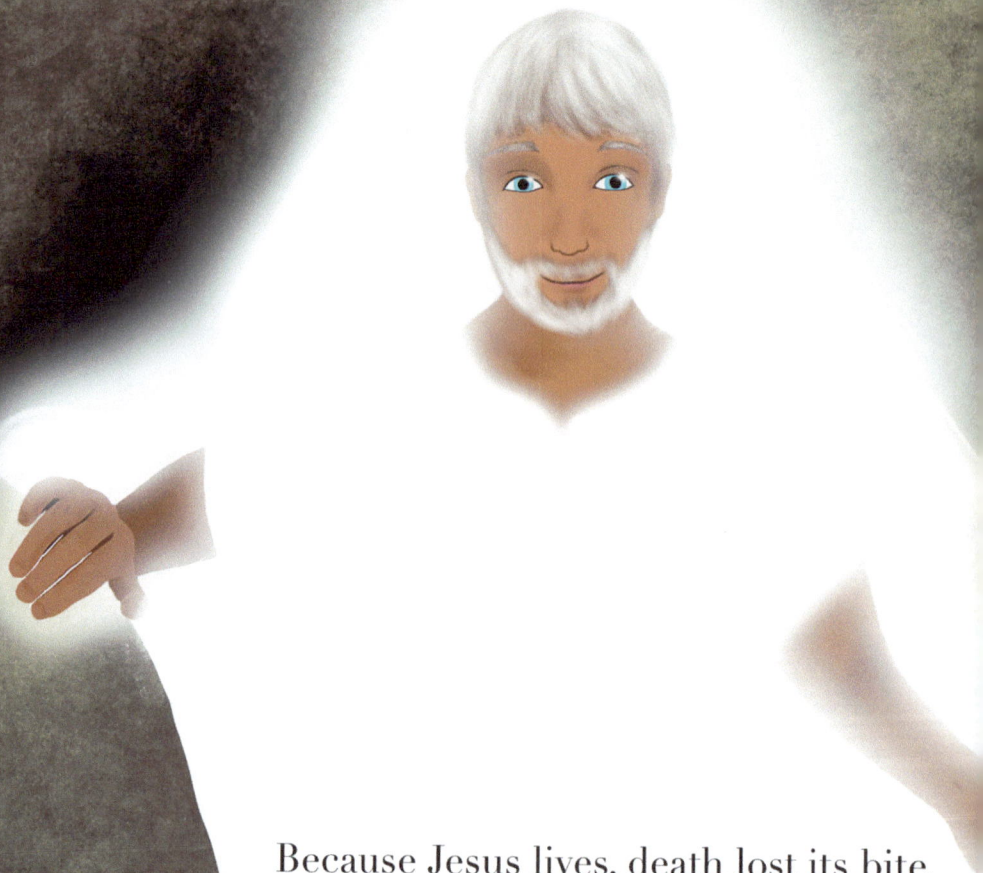

Because Jesus lives, death lost its bite.
And we'll all live again—
we'll be glorious and bright!

We call Him our Savior because He's the way
we can hope to return to the
heavens someday.
For He loves us more than we comprehend,
and His promises aid us
straight through to the end.

When this life is over, we all will live on.

We'll join with our families and friends who've long gone.

A chance will be given for all souls to hear

the plan of their Father who holds them so dear.

For souls with good hearts who gave life their best, the world of spirits is pure peace and rest.

And those who spread evil throughout their Earth days will await with their guilt burning bright as a blaze.

15

We'll all live as spirits 'til
we rise with the sun—

our spirits and bodie[s]
reunited as one!

Then comes our judgment — we'll each go in turn—
to stand before Father with all that we've learned.

He'll gaze on our hearts, over all that we've done,
and take a good measure of who we've become.

And if we've repented, there's nothing to fear;
our Lord and Savior will ever be near.

Then at last we can walk
through the glorious
gates and into the
kingdom where our God
awaits.

A celestial home with
our families together—
a place where our
learning can go on
forever.

A terrestrial world will
exist then as well—

a place where less valiant
people will dwell.

And for those who reject
the truth that they know,

the telestial exists, where
no one can grow.

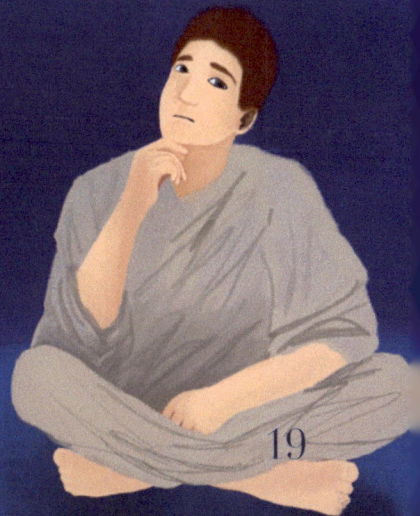

Three kingdoms that differ like the sun,
moon, and stars—

we alone can decide which kingdom is ours.

For we choose with our thoughts, deeds, and desires.
And this is a truth that our Father inspires.

20

He created the plan—
    a spectacular way
for His children to grow
    and be like Him someday.
    So when life seems dreary or too much to comprehend, simply
        remember: you didn't begin here, and it isn't your end.

You're a child of God,

a limitless being with a heart full of light.

Through Christ you can thrive through even the darkest of nights.

Life's paths may seem long,

but your home isn't far.

And if you ask, Father will always remind you exactly who you are.

Scripture References

Life before Earth
- Proverbs 8:22-31
- Jeremiah 1:5
- Moses 3:5
- Abraham 3:22-23

Heavenly parents/children of God
- Acts 17:29
- Romans 8:16
- Hebrews 12:9
- 1 Nephi 17:36
- Moses 1:39

The Creation
- Genesis 1
- Moses 2-3
- Abraham 3:24-25

Adam and Eve
- Genesis 2-3
- 2 Nephi 2

Life on Earth, and our freedom to choose
- Joshua 24:15
- 2 Nephi 2:26-29
- Moroni 7:12-19

Sin, and the way it separates us from God
- Romans 3:23
- Ephesians 5:5
- 3 Nephi 27:19

The doctrine of Jesus Christ is the way home to God
- John 3:16-17
- John 3:5
- 2 Nephi 31
- Alma 11:40

Prayer
- Jeremiah 29:13
- Matthew 6:5-15
- Matthew 7:7-11
- Alma 37:37

The Atonement of Jesus Christ
- John 3:16-17
- 1 John 1-7
- 2 Nephi 2:6-8
- Alma 7:11-13
- Alma 34:8-17

Life after death—the spirit world
- Ecclesiastes 12:7
- 1 Peter 4:6
- Alma 40:11-14

Resurrection
- Luke 24:39
- John 11:25
- 1 Thessalonians 4:16-17
- Alma 40:23

Judgment
- Matthew 12:36
- Romans 14:10
- Mosiah 3:24

Exaltation and the kingdoms of glory
- Matthew 25:34
- 1 Corinthians 15:40-41
- 3 Nephi 28:10
- Doctrine & Covenants 76

To learn more about the truths mentioned
in this book, please visit:
www.churchofjesuschrist.org

And for more information about books
written by Whitney H. Murphy, visit
www.forallourlittleones.weebly.com

About the author

Not so long ago, in a place full of snuggles . . .

Whitney H. Murphy is a mommy who loves her little ones more than words can tell. And her family loves bedtime stories—just like yours! One night, Whitney wanted to read a bedtime story to her children that would help her teach them all about God's plan for them. But there was just one problem: that book didn't exist yet! So, she worked hard to create one herself. Now that book is here for you and your family to enjoy as well.

Whitney and her family live in rural Minnesota, where they love to play in the lakes and take long walks to Grandma's house. When her little ones are asleep, Whitney can be found busily writing fiction stories or illustrating colorful pictures for her next book.

The Murphy family in October of 2020, when Whitney was midway through the creation of this book:

Hey, mommies and daddies! Do you enjoy reading adventurous fiction? Learn more about Whitney's Ages of Claya trilogy at www.memoriesofclaya.com.

www.ingramcontent.com/pod-product-compliance
Lightning Source LLC
Chambersburg PA
CBHW042027090426
42811CB00016B/1775